Carl Bernhard Wadström, Capt Arrhenius

Observations on the Slave Trade

And a description of some part of the coast of Guinea, during a voyage,

made in 1787, and 1788

Carl Bernhard Wadström, Capt Arrhenius

Observations on the Slave Trade
And a description of some part of the coast of Guinea, during a voyage, made in 1787, and 1788

ISBN/EAN: 9783337197087

Printed in Europe, USA, Canada, Australia, Japan

Cover: Foto ©ninafisch / pixelio.de

More available books at **www.hansebooks.com**

ON THE

SLAVE TRADE,

AND A

DESCRIPTION

Of some Part of the

COAST of GUINEA,

DURING

A VOYAGE,

Made in 1787, and 1788, in Company with

Doctor A. SPARRMAN and Captain ARREHENIUS,

BY

C. B. WADSTROM,

Chief Director of the Royal Assay and Refining Office; Member of the Royal Chamber of Commerce, and of the Royal Patriotic Society, for Improving Agriculture, Manufactures, and Commerce in Sweden.

LONDON:

Printed and Sold by James Phillips, George-Yard, Lombard-Street, 1789.

P R E F A C E.

IN communicating to the publick the re-
sult of my obfervations lately made in a
voyage to the Coaft of Guinea, with two of
my countrymen, it is not my intention, without fufficient reafon, to add to the number
of publications which have lately enlightened
Europe, on a fubject fo deferving her attention, and in the impartial inveftigation of
which fhe is fo zealoufly employed.

Animated with a defire of defending the
caufe of fuffering humanity, I have no other
end in view, than that of contributing fome
fmall affiftance to the well concerted plans
of others, by making known what my own
experience has dictated; in a word, to relate
what I have feen, and to fhew, without vain
pretences, what my ideas are, on a plan fo

well

well calculated to expand every heart that is now cherifhing a hope for its fuccefs.

As the fubject has been fo amply treated, my readers will not expect to find novelty in every part of this tract; but having been fo fortunately fituated, as to be enabled fully to inform myfelf of the nature of the flave trade; of the manner in which the negroes are treated by the Europeans; but more particularly of the poffibility of improving, by cultivation, the fruitful foil of Africa, it fhall be my endeavour to treat thefe important fubjects in a manner interefting and new.

In the prefence of the two moft refpectable nations of Europe, would I were endowed with powers to reprefent in colours fufficiently ftriking, the frightful picture I have formed to myfelf, of the above-mentioned traffick, and thereby to prove, that thefe deteftable markets for human flefh, conftitute the laft ftage of all falfe principles; the greateft of all abufes; the inverfion of all order; and originate folely in that
corrupted

corrupted fyſtem of commerce, which per-
vades every civilized nation at this day. In
fact, when the principles of commerce had
been once diverted from the noble *end* of its
inſtitution, an inſtitution which promoted
the free circulation of commodities, the in-
creaſe of knowledge, and the wealth and
profperity of nations, and when the fpirit of
felf-intereſt and monopoly firſt perverted it
from this univerfal end, which ought ever to
have been kept in view, and confined it to
particular nations, following infenfibly the
ſteps of its degradation, it became the mer-
cenary object of individuals, feparate from
the general good; could it then be a matter
of furprize, that it fhould ultimately become
fo debafed, as to regard man himfelf as a
merchandife? This deteſtable abufe may be
confidered as proceeding from a degenerate
love of *dominion*, and *of poſſeſſing* the property of others; which, inſtead of diffuſing
the genial influence of benevolence and
liberty, produces, in their ſtate of inverſion,
all the horrors of tyranny and ſlavery.

Perfuaded

Perfuaded that the moment is now arrived, when mankind will begin to make a real ufe of their great fcientific acquirements, and of the multiplicity of their difcoveries; perfuaded that the evil, which begins to infect mankind, has no other bafis than the execrable traffic, which is at this day fo generally carried on at the expence of human liberty; and convinced at the fame time, of the exiftence of a Providence, which directs all things according to the univerfal end it propofes in its impenetrable decrees, and that we are but inftruments, by whom it executes its great defigns; convinced, I fay, of all thefe important truths, and inflamed with an ardent defire of affifting in the execution of this great and noble attempt, I am not only ready to devote my own perfon in this caufe, but alfo to excite all thofe in whofe breaft there ftill remains a fpark of humanity, to unite with prudence and activity, to accomplifh this grand work, which has for its end the extermination of every *evil* and *falfe* principle, preparing the way for the reception of *Goodnefs* and *Truth*, in every human fociety.

When

When I reflect on the importance, the extent, and the grandeur of this fubject, it gives me pain in being obliged to treat it in fo hafty and incorrect a manner; but preffed for time, I truft my candid readers will receive thefe few hints in good part, allowing for the neceffity of their appearing at this critical moment, when all the great focieties of Europe are fo ftrongly interefting themfelves in the tender caufe of humanity, laudably vying with each other in the honour of pleading at the bar of human fenfibility, in favour of the moft oppreffed nations in the univerfe.

It may be expedient here to inform my readers, that I intend to publifh a more circumftantial account of my voyage to the Coaft of Guinea, when opportunity is afforded to prepare it for publick infpection; wherein I propofe to treat more fully on the geographical defcription of the country, on the manners, laws, and cuftoms of the different nations which inhabit thofe fhores; moreover, to treat concerning the commerce now carried on, but more particularly, on

that

that which may hereafter be eftablifhed with very great advantage. I alfo referve to myfelf the fatisfaction then of informing the public, who was the auguft promoter of the enterprife I undertook, in concert with my two refpectable countrymen, and with what humanity France concurred with him in affifting us to perform the voyage. How providentially I was led to make obfervations on a fubject (I mean the abolition of the flave trade) which could only have been undertaken by a nation of fuch a character and power as that which I have now the honour to addrefs!

In expofing to the world the atrocious acts committed in that part of the globe to which I have been eye-witnefs, it is not improbable, that both the nations and individuals who have countenanced them, may confider the writer in the light of a fpy, and a divulger of thofe things which ought, in honour, to have been buried in filence. But if they can find no other appellation for the juft and pure intentions of a friend to mankind, who dares to expofe crimes and cruelties

ties which the abufers of human right are guilty of, he then accounts it an honour in difcharging the duty he owes to fociety, to be efteemed as fuch. But let it be well obferved, that herein he fpeaks from a refpect due only to truth, with a view to expofe *Wickednefs* and *Falfehood*, but not *Nations* or *Individuals*.

CONTENTS.

CONTENTS.

OBSERVATIONS

ON THE

SLAVE TRADE, &c.

SECT. I.

On the Mode of procuring Slaves.

CHAP. I.

WAR.

AMONG the various fources, from whence the Europeans are fupplied with flaves on the coaft of Africa, I fhall firft reckon that of *War*.

The *Wars* which the inhabitants of the interior parts of the country, beyond Senegal, Gambia, and Sierra Leona, carry on with each

A   other,

other, are chiefly of a predatory nature, and owe their origin to the yearly number of flaves, which the Mandingoes, or the inland traders fuppofe will be wanted by the veffels that will arrive on their coaft. Indeed thefe predatory incurfions depend fo much on the demand for flaves, that if in any one year there be a greater concourfe of European fhips than ufual, it is obferved that a much greater number of captives from the interior parts of the country is brought to market the next.

The unhappy captives, many of whom are people of diftinction, fuch as princes, priefts, and perfons high in office, are conducted by the Mandingoes in droves of twenty, thirty, or forty, chained together, either to Fort St. Jofeph on the river Senegal, or Niger, in the country of Gallam, or to places near the river Gambia. But when the trade with the French on the river Senegal happens to be ftopped, (which was the cafe in 1787) they bring all their captives to the mouth of the Gambia, Sierra Leona, and other places down the coaft. Thefe Mandingoes perform the whole

whole journey, except at certain feafons of the year, when they are met by the traders belonging to the coaft, who receive the flaves from them, and give them the ufual articles of merchandize in exchange.

What I have hitherto faid, was taken from the beft accounts I could collect both from the black and white traders, during my refidence upon the coaft. It is proper, however, that I fhould ftate fomething on this head, that has come within my own knowledge.

The Moors, who inhabit the countries on the north of the River Senegal, are particularly infamous for thefe predatory *Wars*. They crofs the river, and attacking the negroes, bring many of them off. There are not a few who fubfift by means of thefe unprovoked excurfions. The French, to encourage them in it, make annual prefents to the Moorifh kings. Thefe are given them under certain conditions, firft, that their fubjects fhall not carry any of their gum to the Englifh at Portendic; and, fecondly, that

they

they fhall be ready, on all occafions, to furnifh
flaves. To enable them to fulfil this laft article, they never fail to fupply them with
ammunition, guns, and other inftruments of
War.

To confirm what I have now faid, I fhall
put down the following example:

The king of Almammy had, in the year,
1787, very much to his honour, enacted a
law, that no flave whatever fhould be marched
through his territories. At this time feveral French veffels lay at anchor in the Senegal, waiting for flaves. The route of the
black traders in confequence of this edict of
the king, was ftopped, and the flaves carried
to other parts. The French, unable on this
account to complete their cargoes, remon-
ftrated with the king. He was, however,
very unpropitious to their reprefentations,
for he returned the prefents which had been
fent him by the Senegal company, of which
I myfelf was a witnefs; declaring, at the
fame time, that all the riches of that company fhould not divert him from his
defign.

defign. In this fituation of affairs, the French were obliged to have recourfe to their old friends, the Moors. Thefe, who had before fhewn themfelves fo ready on fuch occafions, were no lefs ready and active on this. They fet off in parties to furprife the unoffending negroes, and to carry among them all the calamities of *War*. Many unfortunate prifoners were fent, and for fome time continued to be fent in. I was once curious enough to wifh to fee fome of thofe that had juft arrived. I applied to the Director of the company, who conducted me to the flave-prifons. I there faw the unfortunate captives, chained two and two together, by the foot. The mangled bodies of feveral of them, whofe wounds were ftill bleeding, exhibited a moft fhocking fpectacle; and their fituation may be much eafier conceived than defcribed. The Director of the company, however, ufed his beft endeavours to confole them.

This is a fpecifick inftance, clearly fhewing that *one War at leaft* was undertaken for the fole purpofe of procuring flaves. I

A 3   cannot,

cannot, however, help obferving, that if no fuch inftance as this had come within my knowledge during my ftay in thofe parts, I fhould yet have thought myfelf juftifiable in fuppofing, that the *Wars* among the negroes originated in the flave trade. For in all .the obfervations I have been able to make (and I went to the coaft of Africa, not with any commercial views, but for the fole purpofe of inquiry and obfervation) I have ever confidered the negroes as a quiet, inoffenfive people, happy in themfelves, and in one another, enjoying the comforts of life, without the intervention of toil and trouble. If, therefore, I had found *Wars* among a people of fuch difpofitions, and fo fituated as to have no motive for them, I fhould certainly have fet them down, as having been excited for fome diabolical purpofe, and for none fo likely as for the profecution of the flave-trade.

CHAP. II.

C H A P. II.

P I L L A G E.

A fecond fource, from whence the Europeans are fupplied with flaves on the coaft of Africa, is *Pillage*, which is of two kinds; publick or private. It is publick, when practifed by the direction of the kings, private, when practifed by individuals. I muft alfo make a further diftinction, namely, as it is practifed by the blacks and the whites. This laft I call Robbery, which will be the fubject of the next article.

The publick *Pillage* is, of all others, the moft plentiful fource, from which the flave trade derives its continuance and fupport. The kings of Africa (I mean in that part of the country which I have vifited) incited by the merchandize fhewn them, which confifts principally of ftrong liquors, give orders to their military to attack their own villages in the night. Saturday night is particularly fixed upon for this purpofe, being efteemed

the

the moſt lucky for expeditions of this kind. However, when ſlaves are wanted in haſte, no night is deemed ſo inauſpicious as to prevent an attempt.

As I have been myſelf an eye-witneſs to ſeveral of theſe nocturnal expeditions, it will, perhaps, be better to illuſtrate this kind of *Pillage* by ſome examples.

The French make preſents to the negro as well as the Mooriſh kings. It happened when I was at Goree, that an ambaſſador was to be ſent from thence to the king of Barbeſin on this errand. I obtained leave with my fellow travellers to accompany the embaſſy. We accordingly ſet out, and arrived at Joal, a place where the king reſides at particular times of the year, viz. when the trading veſſels arrive there.

It is uſual, on the receipt of theſe preſents, to ſend back a number of ſlaves in return. It ſo happened, however, that the king of Barbeſin had no ſlaves in his poſſeſſion at that time. This circumſtance it was, that afforded

ed

ed me an opportunity of feeing the expeditions before mentioned.

We refided, I believe, about a week at Joal. During our refidence there, the *Pillage*, of which I have been fpeaking, was attempted almoft every night. The following is a defcription of the perfons concerned in it, and of their various fuccefs.

There were feveral parties of the military, affembled at fix in the evening, or about dufk. Each party confifted of about ten or twelve. A large horfeman's mufket was refted on each of their faddles, in the fame manner as thofe of the Englifh heavy cavalry. On their fhoulders were fufpended a bow, and a quiver full of arrows. Thus equipped, they went to different villages belonging to the king, and returned ufually about five in the morning, or a little before day-light.

In fome of their attempts they returned without a fingle flave. In others they were more fuccefsful. At one time in particular they came back with but one captive. This

was

was a beautiful young negrefs, from one of
the king's own villages. She was immediately delivered, notwithſtanding her tears and
cries, to the French ambaſſador, whom we
accompanied, and, by his order, was carried
on board.

It was fortunate however for her, that ſhe
belonged to one of thoſe families, which, in
conſequence of their birth, are exempted by
the laws of the country from ſlavery. This
occaſioned a commotion; for the action appeared to the minds of the people, to be ſo
unjuſt and repugnant to the eſtabliſhed laws,
that they were nearly on the point of rebel-
ling. The king, when he came to his ſenſes
(for he had given his orders reſpecting the
ſeizure of this girl in a ſtate of intoxica-
tion) ſaw in ſo lively a manner the conſe-
quences of this raſh proceeding, that with
the moſt abject ſubmiſſion, he deſcended to
prayers and intreaties with the owner, to
return the innocent and unfortunate girl.
The Frenchman, though ſurrounded by
more than two thouſand negroes at the time,
and though the embaſſy, including myſelf
and

and fellow-travellers, confifted but of five
white people, was fo madly obftinate, as for
a long time to refufe his requeft ; I fay madly, becaufe in all the adventures of my life,
I had never fo much reafon to be alarmed
for the prefervation of it. At length, after
much intreaty, the king promifed him two
others in exchange, whom he expected to
feize on a future expedition ; and thus was
the unhappy girl reftored to her difconfolate
family.

At another time, the military, who had
been fent out to *Pillage*, returned with feveral
captives. Thefe confifted of men, women,
and children. The men, as they were
brought in, exhibited marks of great dejec-
tion. One of them, however, appeared to
be quite frantick with grief. He befeeched
his captors, with great fervency, that they
would not tear him from his wife and children. The women, on the other hand, vented
their forrow in fhrieks and lamentations. The
children, in a ftate of palpitation, clung to
their mother's breafts. Their little eyes
were fo fwelled with crying, that they could

cry

cry no more. During all this time, the captors, to fhew their joy on the occafion, and
to drown the cries of their unfortunate fel-
low-fubjects, were beating large drums.
To this was added, all the noife that could
be collected from the blowing of horns,
and the human voice. Taking in the
fhrieks and agony of the one, and the fhouts
and joy of the other, with the concomitant
inftruments of noife, I was never before witnefs to fuch an infernal fcene.

What I have faid of the king of Barbefin's
conduct with refpect to the mode of procuring flaves, is equally applicable to thofe other
kings of the country, of whom I have any
knowledge. King Damel, whofe dominions
lie between Portudal and Senegal, wanting
a flave to deliver in exchange for fome goods
he had bargained for with a Goree trader,
ordered his foldiers to feize on one of his
own fubjects. Finding a woman (whofe
hufband was abfent) in a hut with her children, they feized her, bound her, and tore
her from her babes, who were rejected, as
not being able to perform the journey down
to the fhore.

The

The king of Sallum, though he never taftes any fpirituous liquors, has recourfe to the fame practice, as if by the common confent of the kings of Africa, thefe were the meafures to be invariably purfued. The articles, moft in demand with this king, are Spanifh dollars, and Dutch gourds. Both thefe he caufes to be melted down, and then to be worked into chains, bracelets, and other ornaments for himfelf and his favourites. Having fixed an extraordinary value upon thefe, he will at any time depopulate a village to obtain them. Such are the effects of avarice, when it has the power of gratification.

The veffels employed in the trade to lum, by the mulattoes of Goree, are generally floops. With thefe they go up the river, and arrive in about three days. Their ftay there is very uncertain. It is in general from one to four weeks, according as the king is fuccefsful or not in thofe *Pillages* which he attempts for the fake of procuring flaves. When the traders have completed their cargoes, they return to Goree, where they deliver them, in about eight days. The flaves,

flaves, fo delivered, are fhipped off, by the firft opportunity, to the French colonies.

In fpeaking of thefe floops, I cannot refrain from mentioning an inftance which came under my own eye. A trading mulattoe of Goree, whofe name was Martin, had obtained from the king of Sallum, by means of the publick *Pillage* before defcribed, a floop full of captives. The greater part of them were women and children. Notwithftanding this, they had been thrown into the floop as if they had been articles of lumber, and devoid of feeling. Obliged, moreover, from too clofe a ftowage, to lie on the inequalities and protuberances of the bare planks, without being able to change their pofition, they had in the courfe only of eight days (which I ftated to be the time of the paffage from Sallum to Goree) been very materially hurt: for, when I faw them brought out of the floop, they had feveral contufions on various parts of their bodies, and in others their flefh was feverely cut. A poor child in particular, about two years old, had a very deep wound in his fide, made in the manner

above

above ſtated. He lay afterwards, upon being landed, with the wound contiguous to the ground, ſo that the ſand getting into it, put him to exquiſite pain. I mention this inſtance, only to give an idea of what are thought to be rooms of accommodation for ſlaves, and of that inhumanity, which naturally ſprings out of the proſecution of this trade.

Before I cloſe my account of the publick *Pillage,* I muſt not forget to mention, that the kings of thoſe parts, (except the king of Sallum) never openly profeſs the right, which they thus unjuſtly uſurp over the lives and liberties of their ſubjects. For this reaſon they plan their expeditions in ſuch a manner, that they muſt arrive at the place they intend to *Pillage,* in the dead of the night. It is impoſſible, therefore, for their ſubjects, in ſuch a caſe, to diſcover who are the inſtruments of thoſe acts of violence; and they may with greater reaſon ſuppoſe, that they were perpetrated by a roving banditti, than by the direction of their own kings.

I come

I come now to the private *Pillage*. This
is practifed by individuals, who, tempted by
the merchandize brought by the Europeans,
lie in wait for one another. For this purpofe
they befet the roads, and other places, fo that
a travelling negro can hardly ever efcape
them. To enumerate the many inftances
of this private depredation that happen,
would be an endlefs tafk. I fhall therefore
felect but one, which, on account of the
circumftances that followed, may ftrike the
reader as fingular.

A Moor had feized a free negro, and,
having fecured him, he brought him to Senegal, and fold him to the company. A few
days afterwards this moor was taken by fome
negroes in the fame manner, and brought
to be fold in his turn. The company feldom buy moors: but as they were obliged,
in confequence of their privileges, to fupply
the colony of Cayenne with a certain number
of flaves, and as feveral fhips then in the
road, in confequence of the king of Almammy's edict, as before related, could not complete their cargoes, they made the lefs fcruple

to

to buy him on this occasion. Chance so directed, that the moor, after he had been purchased, was carried on board the same ship, in which the negro lay. They no sooner met, than a quarrel took place between them, which occasioned, for some days, a great tumult in the veffel. Such rencounters frequently happen in the slave-ships, and the uproars, occasioned by them, are seldom or never quieted, till some mischief has been done.

CHAP. III.

Of ROBBERY.

I have been hitherto describing the *Pillage*, as it is either publick or private. I have also considered it as practised by the blacks upon one another. I come now to speak of it, as it is practised upon these by the whites; and this I call *Robbery*.

It is too well known, at least on some parts of the coaft, that the Europeans have

B not

not failed, when opportunity prefented itfelf, to feize the unfufpicious natives of
Africa, and to carry them by force to their
own colonies.

This is ufually practifed by the Europeans,
where they have no fettlements ; fo that the
fact generally efcapes the notice of their
countrymen ; I mean principally up the
rivers, where they have ventured to pene-
trate for the purpofe of a more advantageous trade. At fuch places, they compel
the negroes to deliver them hoftages, whom
they keep on board. The truce being concluded, the unfufpicious natives embark with
confidence, and repeatedly vifit the veffel
without any kind of fufpicion or fear. But,
if the wind fhould be at all favourable, none
of the European monfters, who are engaged
in this trade, fcruple to fet fail, and to
carry away not only the free negroes, who
have come on board to trade, but the hoftages alfo, in defiance of the law of nations
and common honefty.

Thefe

Thefe tranfactions are not only iniquitous in themfelves, and therefore derogatory from the character of a civilized nation, but are often fo fatal in their confequences, that thofe, who perpetrate them, have a claim to the appellation of devils rather than men. For it may eafily be fuppofed, that the relations and friends of thofe, who have been thus fraudulently carried off, will fpare no pains to retaliate. This is generally the cafe. The next fhip that vifits the coaft, is perhaps cut off. Thus, to a villainous action, is fuperadded the guilt of becoming inftrumental to the murder perhaps of their own countrymen, and at any rate of occafioning the innocent to undergo the punifhment of the guilty.

When I was at Goree, in the year 1787, accounts came down by fome French merchantmen from the Gambia of the following particulars.

The captain of an Englifh fhip, which had been fome time in that river, had enticed feveral of the natives on board, and, finding

a favourable

a favourable opportunity, failed away with them. His veffel however was, by the direction of Providence, driven back to the coaft from whence it had fet fail, and was obliged to caft anchor on the very fpot where this act of treachery had been committed. At this time two other Englifh veffels were lying in the fame river. The natives, ever fince the tranfaction, had determined to retaliate. They happened, at this juncture, to be prepared. They accordingly boarded the three veffels, and, having made themfelves mafters of them, they killed moft of their crews. The few who efcaped to tell the tale, were obliged to take refuge in a neighbouring French factory. Thus did the innocent fuffer the fame punifhment as the guilty; for it did not appear that the crews of the other two veffels had been at all concerned in this villainous meafure.

Thefe particulars, as I obferved before, had found their way down to us at Goree, and, from the channels through which they came, I had no reafon to queftion their truth.

It

It is remarkable, however, that, though I wanted no confirmation of them in my own mind, yet, fince my arrival in London, I have heard them fully fubftantiated : for I dined lately by accident with a certain underwriter, to whom úndefignedly relating the time, place, and other circumftances of this tranfaction, I found that I had only been defcribing the fate of certain veffels, which, to his knowledge, had been cut off in the fame part of the world, and at the fame feafon,

B 3   CHAP.

CHAP. IV.

Of TREACHERY or STRATAGEM.

The various other ways in which flaves are obtained, may be included under the words *Treachery* or *Stratagem*, being only fo many different modes of the fame practice. One or two inftances will, I hope, fuffice, as I do not wifh to take up the reader's time more than is neceffary, and as he will be enabled by them to judge of the reft. Befides, the ftratagems which the traders daily practife to get flaves, are fo numerous, that it would take a volume to recount them.

A French merchant of Goree landing at a village, obferved an handfome well-made negro. He immediately made application to the chief of the village to feize him. On the propofal of the chief, the people unanimoufly agreed to grant his requeft:

queft: for it is a law in thofe parts, that if all the village confent, any vifitor refiding among them may be made a flave. To gain the confent of a whole village on fuch an occafion, is by no means difficult. The Africans in general, like other people in the fame unimproved ftate, are governed by their paffions, and the prince has only to diftribute a fufficient quantity of fpirituous liquors among them to produce the effect he wifhes for. Such was the cafe in the prefent inftance; and the unfortunate negro, though he was their neighbour and vifitor, was taken and fent into flavery. His wife, having heard of his capture, came down bathed in tears. She begged to be bought, that fhe might go with him, and fhare his fate. But the dealer who bought him, had probably no goods at the time, and her intreaties were ineffectual.

The king of Sallum, under pretence of wanting millet, enticed from a neighbouring village a negrefs, who had a quantity to dif-pofe of. Elated with the profpect of fell-

ing

ing it to advantage, she did not consider the imprudence of the step she was about to take. She accordingly went to the king, who not only immediately deprived her of her millet, but seized her, and sold her for a slave.

I cannot close my account of the different methods daily practised to obtain slaves, without giving an instance, that will shew, in a very glaring light, the bad tendency of the slave trade, and the baneful effects it produces on the human heart.

One of the Moorish kings had received from the director of the company of Senegal, the predecessor of him who now occupies that post, the usual presents, in consequence of which he was bound to procure slaves. Having been rather dilatory in the performance of his engagement, he was applied to by the director, who represented to him the pressing wants of the company. The king, thus urgently pressed, offered him a certain negro on account. This negro was none other than his own minister, who had been his confidential
friend

friend and faithful advifer for many years. The director,' fhocked at the circumftance, endeavoured to point out to him the impropriety of his conduct, but his reprefentations were ineffectual. The negro, in whofe prefence the offer was made, finding that his unworthy mafter was obftinately bent upon his defign, ran up to him, drew his dagger, and plunging it into his own breaft, exclaimed, " Thou favage! I fhall have the fatisfaction of expiring, before thou canft reap any advantage from thy bafe ingratitude to the beft of fervants."

I have now finifhed my fection on the mode of procuring flaves, and I fhould have been made much happier by my vifit to the coaft of Africa, if no fuch inftances had occurred, as I have felt myfelf obliged to communicate to the reader.

SECT.

S E C T. II.

Of the Manner in which the Negroes are treated by the Europeans.

C H A P. I.

Of the Negroes confidered as TRADERS.

Self-intereft, the principle of all commerce, appears in the very bafeft point of view, when confidered, with a reference to the intercourfe fubfifting between the white and the black nations. The fraud and violence which the ftronger generally imagine they have a right in trade to exercife towards the weaker, compel the latter in their turn to have recourfe to practices equally bafe and cruel. Such is the true picture of the low cunning and barbarity which the whites practife towards the negroes, and thefe laft towards their own people.

In

In fuch myfteries of iniquity, the Europeans have a decided advantage over the untu-
tored African nations; and thus practife their
villainous artifices with impunity. The moft
defpicable juggling tricks are ufed in meafur-
ing or reckoning the commodities bartered
with the negroes. Thus for example, inftead
of the bottles and barrels fhewn and ap-
proved of, others are fubftituted apparently
of the fame fize, but containing lefs perhaps
by one half. Advantage is taken of the
difficulty with which the negroes reckon beyond ten, and thus the accounts are confu-
fed, and they are deprived of the greater part
of the commodities bargained for. The wine
and fpirits, famples of which the negroes
had tafted pure, are afterwards adulterated
with water. They are defrauded in all forts
of weights and meafures; and, that the European adepts in villainy may play off their
tricks with fuccefs, they previoufly take care
to intoxicate the unfufpecting negroes, and
by this means fafcinate their fenfes in
fuch a manner, as to multiply or mag-
nify every article fet before them. Thefe
ways of trading are efteemed the moft modeft
that

that can be practifed, and there is not a fingle European who fcruples in the leaft to
have recourfe to them on all occafions. I
have repeatedly been an eye-witnefs of fuch
villainy.

C H A P.   II.

Of the Negroes confidered as SLAVES.

On the coaft of Africa there are two defcriptions of flaves, namely, the immediate
defcendants of flaves, and thofe who are reduced to flavery in the different ways I have
defcribed. The former are feldom fold, except for theft, but the moft trivial tranfgref-
fion of this kind is often made a pretext for
felling them. At Goree I was prefent at
feveral publick fales of young women,* who
were fold for acts of petty larceny, which
fcarcely deferved the name of crimes. The
treatment thefe laft experience is mild, when
compared to that of the wretches, who are
enflaved by force or fraud, and who are treat-

* The treatment the fex experience from the white traders on all occafions, is fuch, as decency forbids me to
defcribe.

ed

ed exactly like wild beasts. They are confined in prisons or dungeons, resembling dens, where they lie naked on the sand, crowded together and loaded with irons. In consequence of this cruel mode of confinement, they are frequently covered with cutaneous eruptions. Ten or twelve of them feed together out of a trough, precisely like so many hogs. There is even less care taken of them than of brutes, while they are confined in these horrid receptacles, and, till they are stowed away in the slave vessels, to be sent from the coast; nor are they worse treated on board, if we may credit some accounts.

I am very sorry that humanity obliges me here to divulge a most barbarous practice, frequently used by the French traders in the Middle Passage. I have been assured by several of their merchants and captains, that when detained by calms, or contrary winds, occasioning a shortness of provisions and water; or when some fatal disease happens to break out among the slaves, they never fail to mix corrosive sublimate, or some other active

poison

poifon with their victuals, and thus cooly dif-
patch the wretches committed to their charge.
They affirm that it would be an act of imprudence to undertake fuch a voyage unpro-
vided with poifonous drugs, and they boaft
of being lefs cruel than the Dutch and the
Englifh, who in fimilar circumftances throw
the innocent victims over-board without cere-
mony.*

Of the above cruel practice, my journal
furnifhes a melancholy inftance, communi-
cated to me by Capt. L. of Havre de Grace.
About two years ago, a flave veffel belonging
to Breft, having been becalmed in the Middle
Paffage, fell fhort of provifions and water.
The Captain on this occafion had recourfe to
poifon, by which fo great a number was daily
difpatched, that of *five hundred* flaves, only
twenty-one arrived at Cape François.

* Since my arrival in London, this horrid practice has been
authenticated by the refpectable authority of feveral French
gentlemen.

SECT.

S E C T. III.

Whether the Negroes are naturally inclined to Induſtry.

C H A P. I.

In FOREIGN COUNTRIES.

From ſeveral experiments made on different plantations in the Weſt-Indies, it appears, that negroes, when working, not by
the day, but by taſk, have given convincing
proofs both of ability and induſtry.*

C H A P. II.

In THEIR OWN COUNTRY.

As liberty and reaſon, the two grand
ſprings of all human action, are not yet

* A remarkable and well authenticated proof of the
above intereſting fact will be given at the end of this little
tract.

developed

developed in thefe people, who have long
remained in a ftate of infancy, folely becaufe
their faculties have not been cultivated, in
confequence of which their wants have
been but few, it may perhaps be concluded,
that thefe raw nations are incapable of civilization, but this opinion will foon vanifh
on reflecting, that the effects produced
muft entirely depend on the manner of
forming their intellect. New objects ought
to be prefented to them, in order to excite
new defires, and to call forth thofe faculties, which have hitherto lain dormant,
merely for want of exercife. Thus in the
progrefs of their improvement it will be
neceffary to introduce among them a pro-
portionable degree of what we generally call
luxury, by which I do not mean the abufe
of the conveniences of life, which enervates
mankind, but fuch moderate ufe of thofe
conveniences, as will roufe them to action.

The behaviour of the king of Barbefin
convinced me, that this ufeful degree of
luxury might eafily be introduced among the
people of the coaft. I gave him a pair of
common

common enamelled flave buttons, with which, though ignorant of their ufe, he was infinitely delighted. On my fhewing him for what purpofe they were intended, he appeared much mortified that his fhirt had no button-holes; but obferved that it differed in this refpect from that of a mulatto from Goree, with whom he infifted on exchanging fhirts in our prefence, a demand with which the man was forced to comply. Tranfported with his new ornaments, the king held up his hands to difplay them to the people. His courtiers foon furrounded my hut, intreating me to furnifh them alfo with buttons, which I did with pleafure. This fondnefs of the natives for European baubles, proves that an advantageous commerce might be eftablifhed among them with very little trouble and expenfe.

The conduct of the prefent king (late grand marabou*) of Almammy, is more interefting to humanity, and evinces the firm manly character of the negroes when en-

* The marabous are the chief priefts among the negroes, and are the only people who can read and write Arabic.

lightened.

lightened. His underſtanding having been more cultivated in his youth than that of the other black princes, he has rendered himſelf intirely independent of the whites. He has not only prohibited the ſlave-trade throughout his dominions, but (in the year 1787) would not ſuffer the French to march their captives from Gallam, through his country. He redeems his own ſubjects when ſeized by the Moors, and encourages them to raiſe cattle, to cultivate the land, and to practiſe all kinds of induſtry. As grand marabou, he abſtains from ſtrong liquor, which, however, is not the general rule among that order; for ſome who travel with the whites are not ſcrupulous in this reſpect. His ſubjects, imitating his example, are much more ſober than their neighbours.

This proves to what degree of civilization theſe people might be brought, if with prudence and patience this great and noble enterprize was once undertaken; but without introducing ſome degree of what we generally call Luxury, this cultivation would, in my opinion, be intirely impracticable. To
what

what purpofe would the human underftanding be cultivated, if Luxury, by which I mean nothing more than the improvement of the conveniencies and comforts of life, did not keep pace with it ? The former indeed could not take place without the latter. Uncivilized nations in general are led merely by animal inftinct to procure their fubfiftence, but as foon as the underftanding begins to be enlightened, by means of reflection upon what is agreeable to life, above mere neceffaries, Luxury muft of courfe be introduced.*

* By LUXURY, I underftand, all enjoyments beyond the neceffaries of mere animal life. Confequently to live in a civilized community is already a fort of luxury; and if the cultivation of our underftanding be neceffary, we ought alfo to be indulged in the ufe of a word which is now fo generally abufed.

DESCRIPTION of the COAST.

C H A P. I.

C L I M A T E.

The climate of the coaft of Guinea, as of other countries, varies with the nature of the foil, its elevation or depreffion, the comparative ftate of its improvement, and other circumftances, perhaps not yet fufficiently inveftigated. The latitude of the place is by no means a certain criterion of its climate, fince even in the midft of the torrid zone, we meet with all poffible gradations of climate. The high lands of Camarons in particular, though only between three and four degrees diftant from the line, are covered with ever-lafting fnow.

It is the general opinion, that the moft unhealthy climates on the coaft, are thofe of Senegal and Juda, or, as it is called by the Englifh, Whidah. The neighbourhood of the banks of the River Gambia, however, which

which has lately been much frequented, hath
been found to be as unhealthy as thofe juft
mentioned, efpecially during the great rains,
and immediately after their ceffation. In
general it may be concluded, that low and
marfhy fituations are very unfavourable to
the health of the Europeans, who may expect the moft fatal confequences from irre-
gularity, or excefs of any kind. But a due
regard to temperance, and fuch moderate
exercife as would not induce too violent a per-
fpiration, would doubtlefs be the beft means
of guarding againft the effects of a fudden
change of climate. Thus the body would
gradually accommodate itfelf to its new fituation, as is actually experienced by every one
who duly attends to thefe precautions ; and
this happy effect takes place fooner or later,
according to the weaknefs or ftrength of the
ftranger's conftitution, as well as to the more
or lefs manly education he may have received,
and the habits he may have formed in the
earlier part of his life. The intemperature of
thofe climates may alfo be in fome degree re-
fifted, by fixing one's habitation on an elevated
fpot during the unhealthy feafon of the year.
For my own part, although I arrived on the

coaft

coaft during that feafon, I efcaped all the difeafes of the country. This I afcribe entirely
to the cautious temperance I obferved. During
a mortality which raged at Senegal while I
was there, not a fingle gentleman or officer
on fhore was attacked, but out of eleven fai-
lors belonging to the veffel in which I returned to Europe, fix were taken off in the
fpace of a month. It muft be obferved, however, that feamen, by the tyranny or neglect
of the captains, by a bad or fcanty diet, and
by the other hardfhips they undergo, are often expofed to many caufes of difeafe, which
do not affect perfons living regularly on
fhore, and which will ever more or lefs attend the fervice of monopolizing Companies,
or individual merchants, who, *regardlefs of
the lives of men*, make gain the fole object of
their fpeculations.* It is remarked, that Europeans of a flender habit are generally found
to be the moft healthy on the coaft of Guinea.

From what I have been able to collect, it
appears, that the rainy feafons follow the paffage

* It is worthy of remark, that fince wine was fubftituted
for the brandy, which till within thefe laft three years was
ferved out to the French troops on the coaft, they have been
incomparably healthier.

fage of the fun from the equator to either tropic, fo as always to prevail in thofe places
where the fun is vertical. Eaft of Cape
Palmas I am told they feldom fet in before
June, when the fun returns from the northern
tropic; but to the weftward of that Cape,
and up the whole country, thofe feafons generally commence within the month of May,
and continue for three or four months. In
the beginning of this feafon, the earth being
foftened with the rain, the negroes till and
fow their ground, and after the return of dry
weather, they gather in their crops, an occu-
pation they feldom abandon, even though
allured by the moft advantageous commerce.
I have fufficient reafon to believe, that were
the coaft cultivated to the extent of which
the foil in general is fufceptible, the climate
would be much meliorated.

C H A P. II.

Of the Soil.

The foil all along the coaft is very une-
qual. From Cape Blanco down the coaft,
to the River Gambia, it is in general very

fandy,

fandy, but as the fand confifts of broken fhells, covered in many places with a rich black mould, it muft be favourable to vegetation. The moft barren places of this part of the country, except juft on the fea fhore, are covered with grafs and bufhes; and where the black mould is found, the vegetation is luxuriant, and the trees of vaft dimenfions. I have remarked, that the mountains are generally compofed more or lefs of regular bafaltes, exhibiting remains of moft prodigious volcanoes, the eruptions of which greatly improve the foil around them. Hence the mountains and high grounds at Cape Emanuel, Goree, Cape Rouge, and other places lower down, are commonly very fertile. Where rice thrives beft, the ground in general is low, marfhy, and unhealthy.

C H A P. III.
The Productions.

Animal. The cattle on the coaft are fmaller than thofe of Europe, and not fo fat as thofe of England or Holland; yet their flefh is very nourifhing, and they give milk in abundance,

abundance. Their inferiority appeared to me to be the effect of the carelefs and unfkilful management of the negroes. I once faw four oxen fold for eighteen livres. They muft be raifed on the coaft, as foreign cattle do not thrive. Even thofe from the Cape de Verd Iflands do not anfwer on the coaft. The whole coaft is abundantly ftocked with fheep, hogs, and all forts of poultry, which propagate with aftonifhing rapidity. Fifhing and hunting are moft eagerly purfued by the negroes, who have, however, but a very grofs idea of any mechanical means of facilitating thofe employments. Of the prodigious fhoals of numberlefs kinds of fifh, I could have formed no idea without having feen them with my own eyes. Spermaceti whales abound on the coaft. In pafling from Goree to the Continent, diftant about five miles, I have often rowed through fhoals of them, and have been under no fmall apprehenfions of their overfetting my canoe. Lower down the coaft the Englifh and Portugueze carry on a confiderable fifhery of thofe whales; and ambergris is found in fuch quantities on the coaft, that I have more than once feen the negroes pay their canoes with

it.

it. Till lately the learned were at a lofs to which of the kingdoms of nature this pro-duction was to be referred, but they are now pretty generally agreed, that it is the excre-ment of the fparmaceti whales.

Vegetable. The grafs is thick, and grows to a great height. The natives are often obliged to burn it, to prevent the wild beafts from harbouring in the fields, but it foon fprings up again. Millet, rice, potatoes, pulfe, and many other excellent vegetables, are cultivated on the coaft with very little trouble, and in a profufion perfectly aftonifh-ing to an European. Such indeed is the plenty which prevails on the coaft, that all the European fhips are victualled, without the fmalleft inconvenience to the inhabitants. There is alfo abundance of the moft whole-fome and delicious fruit; articles of no lefs confequence than thofe juft mentioned. Sugar-canes grow wild in many places, which with a little cultivation might be rendered extremely valuable and productive. The fame may be faid of the tobacco-plant. Se-veral fpecies of cotton are alfo fpontaneoufly produced by this excellent foil; one of them

may

may be spun without being carded, and almoft without any preparation. The negroes spin it into very fine yarn, of which they make a good but narrow cloth.*

Indigo of different kinds alfo grows wild, and in fuch quantities, as to be a very troublefome weed in the rice and millet fields. What a ftrange inverfion of nature does not man, actuated by the moft extravagant and moft ridiculous felfifhnefs, every where labour to effect? What neceffity is there for exiling this plant from the foil and climate which nature has affigned it, in order to tranfplant it into a country, where it is far from thriving fo well as in its native place, and where it fails every third or fourth year? Dyers, who have tried the African indigo, affirm, that it is better than that which is produced in Carolina and in the Weft Indies. The fpecimens of cotton and indigo, which I have brought with me from the coaft, have been carefully examined by people of fkill, and found to be of the beft quality.

Gum

* The firft confiderable exportation of cotton and indigo from the Coaft to Europe, as far as I have been informed, was made in the year 1787, while I was at Goree, by a Frenchman, who had refided fome time in that ifland.

Gum is another valuable article, and is not as some imagine produced in the neighbourhood of Senegal only; it is also found on most parts of the coast, though the negroes have not yet got into the practice of collecting it, which they might do with very little trouble. My fellow-traveller, Dr. Sparrman, extracted a large quantity of the sap of a small but most juicy tree, which grows in great abundance on the coast, and exposing it to the sun for a few hours, had the satisfaction to find it converted into an elastic gum, equal in all respects to that which is known by the name of Indian rubber. The coast also produces a great variety of the most valuable and beautiful woods, many of which are scarcely known even to our botanists. I brought with me samples of fourteen species, including one remarkable for its colour, which is a very beautiful red. Among the different plants, which grow on the coast, is a kind of aloes, of which the negroes make most excellent ropes. Of several sorts of roots and leaves they make mats and baskets, and their manufactures of this kind are really elegant;—this being the principal art in which they appear to equal if not to excel the Europeans.

Minerals.

Minerals. —— Except fome trifling and unfuccefsful attempts, made by Chevalier de la Brue, in the beginning of this century, the Europeans have never made any particular fearch for *Minerals* on the coaft, which, however, it would be well worth while to attend to, efpecially as it is well known in what abundance gold is found in the inland parts, notwithftanding the negroes are very unfkilful in collecting it. An exact and regular examination of the metallick productions of the mountains, particularly thofe of Sierra Leona, and the adjacent country, would certainly be an object of great importance. In Gallam is found a very tough and excellent kind of iron, and the negroes work it with much ingenuity.*

* The mineralogical obfervations made by my fellow-traveller, Capt. Arrhenius, on that part of the coaft where we travelled, particularly refpecting the Volcanoes, will undoubtedly prove very interefting, when he has leifure to put them in proper order for publication.

OBSERVATION.——*I cannot omit to mention in this place, that Mr. Geoffroy de Villeneuve, a young French officer, and fkilful naturalift, who made a very extenfive journey in the year* 1787 *into the interior parts of the country above Goree, will probably foon entertain the publick with a faithful defcription thereof, fo much the more interefting, as he has with indefatigable pains and deep knowledge, examined the difpofition of the inhabitants, and the nature of the country, in a manner which certainly will do honour to the philofophy of this century.*

SECT. V.

S E C T. V.

Of the IMPEDIMENTS which will oppose European Settlements on the Coast of Guinea.

C H A P. I.

False Opinions.

The diminution of the value of the West Indian Iſlands will undoubtedly be the ſtrongeſt objection againſt forming ſettlements on the coaſt of Guinea; but this objection, which is wholly reſolvable into a narrow policy, founded on falſe and intereſted principles, might be eaſily obviated, if my neceſſary brevity would permit me to enter on the diſcuſſion. To ſuppoſe that the European nations, which have Weſt Indian colonies, would be injured by forming others in Africa, is juſt as unreaſonable, as to ſuppoſe, that a man's property would

be

be injured by putting him in poffeffion of
another eftate, in addition to that which he
already enjoys. Allow the old colonies to
be leffened in their value, the lofs will be
more than compenfated to the mother
country, by fettlements formed in an extenfive region, which yields fpontaneoufly
the tropical productions now fo much
wanted in all luxurious and civilized com-
munities. I met the whole force of this
objection on the coaft, and perceived clearly
that this circumftance alone had hitherto
prevented the European governments from
forming fettlements in Africa. I neverthelefs faw that fuch fettlements would be
formed fooner or later, and that they could
not fail to acquire ftrength, and to produce
the moft folid advantages to any nation
poffeffed of them, efpecially to that which
fhall firft undertake fo beneficial an enterprize.*

But

* That it is neceffary for a *free*, *commercial*, and *laborious*
nation to look out for foreign fettlements, when *population*
and *manufactured products* encreafe in a fimilar proportion,
is a truth as evident as that without *enlarging fpace* for the
former,

But if even the beft monarchs be furrounded by courtiers, devoted to· partial and avaricious views, under the illufive femblance of national intereft, can it be expected that the light of enlarged policy, diffipating the thick darknefs in which they are enveloped, will difpofe them to adopt plans extenfively beneficial to mankind, and conformable to the great law of creation ?

Are

former, and *feeking for an emporium* for the latter, the progrefs of *population* and *commerce* muft neceffarily and of courfe ceafe. Hence found policy dictates that the government of fuch a nation fhould with the affectionate care of a provident father, prepare proper places for receiving the fuperabundance of population and products — a principle which few mother countries feem to have obferved in the fettlement of colonies. In a future treatife the author will endeavour to fhew, that this fundamental miftake is the true caufe of the ruinous and unfupportable expence in which all the European colonies have involved their refpective mother countries. He will propofe a plan, the adoption of which he is of opinion would effectually prevent fuch ruinous confequences in any fettlement that may hereafter be eftablifhed by the Europeans. He will alfo enumerate the productions of the coaft of Guinea, and the European commodities preferred by the inhabitants, adding fome directions and cautions proper to be obferved in trading and converfing with them, together with feveral other interefting particulars.

Are not the governments of the two moſt
flouriſhing nations, England and France,
who give laws to the reſt of Europe, influenced by powerful poſſeſſors of the ancient
colonies and opulent merchants of their productions? It is impoſſible that informa-
tion of ſo delicate a nature ſhould be obtained pure and unadulterated through the
medium of ſurly, ſordid planters and ſugar
factors, who are acting only from a vile
ſelf-intereſt.*

* I cannot help here reflecting on the ſtrange means the
French employ for the encouragement of this execrable
trade. They allow their merchants a bounty of 150 livres
tournois for each ſlave they import into *Cayenne* and *La
Guyenne* Françoiſe; 100 livres for the ſouthern parts of *St.
Domingo*; 80 livres for *La Jeremie* and its dependencies;
60 livres for *St. Marie*, *Leogane*, and *Port au Prince*; and
50 livres for *Cape François* and its dependencies.—Beſides
this, Government pays a premium of 40 livres per ton for
all the ſhips that go to the coaſt, and they are alſo more
favoured in the meaſurement than any other. Theſe boun-
ties, granted for promoting the ſale of human fleſh, is the
occaſion of their committing the moſt abominable abuſes,
which cry for vengeance, and are even injurious in tho
extreme to the Government which encourages them.

CHAP.

C H A P. II.

Of the Diseases.

The diseases to which the Europeans are subject from the climate of the coast, may be reckoned among the greatest inconveniences to establishments of white people in that part of the world. Fortunately, however, they may in general be obviated by making choice of elevated situations, and if possible by forming the first settlement on an island; by keeping up the spirits of the new colonists, so that their minds may be agreeably occupied to gratify the affections of the soul; by accustoming them, as I have already observed, to a moderate degree of exercise; guarding carefully against wet and damps in the rainy seasons; by observing a good diet, or regularity of living, and keeping the bowels open. Such precautions are the surest antidotes against most of the bad effects usually resulting from a sudden change of climate. It is a fact confirmed by observation, that, excepting accidental or violent

deaths

deaths or infections, diforders to which every country as well as Africa are fubject, the evils I have been fpeaking of, prevail chiefly among that clafs of people, who fuffer their brutal paffions to get the upper hand of their reafon, and whofe will and affections always govern their intellectual faculties. Nothing is more common and fatal among this clafs, than excefs in drinking. Neverthelefs there are remedies on the fpot well known among the negroes, which effectually cure the difeafes that cannot be efcaped.

CHAP. III.

Of Mufketoes.

The mufketoes are generally very troublefome ; but as they are only generated in ftagnant and putrid water, it is eafy to perceive that this evil is not without a remedy; becaufe by draining the marfhes, and by cultivating the land, the caufe which produces them will in a great meafure be removed. It is likewife certain, that it is not difficult to accuftom one's-felf to them, and it is aftonifhing to fee with what unconcern the ne-

groes

groes walk quite naked, furrounded by
fwarms of thofe infects, without regarding
their attacks. Smoke, in general, is a good
prefervative againft them. *

CHAP. IV.

Of Thorns and Thiftles.

The inconveniences of thorns and thiftles
that grow wild in very great abundance
among the trees, bufhes, and grafs, are
likewife an hindrance to the commence-
ment of cultivation; but if the negroes
were employed to pull them up, this ob-
ftacle would be of little confequence; for
they are fo ufed and accuftomed to them,
that they make no fcruple of penetrating
acrofs the thickets which moft abound with
them. Befides, the cultivation of the country will foon exterminate thefe impediments,
as well as many others.

* Mr. Sefstrom, in Sweden, has lately difcovered, that
a very fmall quantity of camphire, ftrewed on a fire-coal,
immediately deftroys every infect within the reach of its
effluvia, and no doubt would prove fatal to the mufketoes.
See the Acts of the Royal Society of Sciences at Stock-
holm, for the year 1787.

S E C T. VI.

R E F L E C T I O N S.

From all that has been faid, as well as
from many other particulars, unneceffary to
be repeated here, as they are already laid before the publick, it is evident, that the flave-
trade is a *Commerce*, carried to the higheft
pitch of human depravity, and it is to be
feared that its total fuppreffion by all the
Europeans nations is a thing more to be
wifhed for than expected at once, unlefs fome
of the civilized nations were to unite in
eftablifhing colonies on the coaft of Guinea.
May therefore every nation, ferioufly engaged
in the caufe of liberty, confider this efficacious
remedy with the ftricteft attention, and reap
the great advantage to be derived from the
fruitful foil of this vaft part of the globe,
by the effectual means already pointed out,

D 3

namely,

namely, that of Cultivation *. But, as the
fettling of new colonies, and the gradual
abolition of this trade, require the moft
fcrupulous attention, I venture to flatter
myfelf, that from fome experience and application to this matter, I fhall be able to
excite every feeling and difinterefted mind, to
view this grand object in a proper point of
light: I confider it therefore as a duty to
lay before them the following reflections.

Though it be ufual to compare nations and
their

* Eftablifhments of new colonies in Africa have been
oppofed by fome with an apparent ftrength of argument;
the principal points of which may be collected under the
following heads: 1ft. That it would be introducing among
the fimple and innocent people the corrupted manners of
the Europeans.—2d. That fuch eftablifhments would be the
means of increafing and perpetuating the practice of making
flaves.—3d. That Government will be expofed to confiderable facrifices to fecure protection to the colonies, and to
fupply them with neceffaries from Europe, &c.—In a work
I am preparing to lay before the publick, it is my intention
to fubmit, for candid perufal, the reflections I have made on
thefe objections, and endeavour to prove the great error by
which thefe real friends to humanity are at prefent influenced.

their colonies to parents and their children, yet in reality the comparifon is not juft, as things are circumftanced at prefent.

In every individual family, what is fo highly regarded, or efteemed fo highly in-terefting, fo ufeful, directing the attention to found policy, as the human production or propagation of mankind? Where is that parent, who not only ftrives to give his children as good an education as he himfelf has received, but impelled by affection even endeavours to elevate them into a fuperior ftate? Acting thus, has he any other end than that of introducing them as active, zealous, and laborious citizens, from a prin-ciple of ufefulnefs, as reafonable, beneficent, and religious fathers of future families, into that fociety, of which he himfelf forms a part?

From what has been faid it follows, that children, when they arrive at the age of maturity, although they have been ufeful to their parents during their minority; yet it is not to be inferred, that from a principle of

obligation

obligation or falfe gratitude, they ought in-
feparably to abide by their parents throughout
life. No! in a more advanced age, nature
and reafon combine to emancipate and juftify
them, even though oppofed by their parents;
when in their turn they independently efta-
blifh themfelves, and lay a foundation for
new families, which augmenting the profperity, and ftrength of the community, neceffarily promotes thofe of their parents.
How could any fociety whatever otherwife
continue to exift? In a word, a child is
fruit hanging on the tree;—man, arrived to
full growth, is feparated therefrom, which,
under the direction of Providence, repro-
duces in its turn, a new tree that may do
honour to the foreft.

The gratitude and filial attachment which
a child conftantly preferves for thofe who
gave him being, is always proportioned to the
education he has received from them, and to
the tie which has been mutually formed on
both fides, during the ftate of non-age.

Societies at large ought to act precifely on the fame principle in forming colonies, fince thefe are nothing elfe but their own children, or the fuperfluity of their population.

When therefore a large Society thus gives birth to a fmall one, in the eftablifhing thereof, can it poffefs a more noble view than that of regarding in the firft place the intereft of mankind, or *univerfal Society*, and afterwards the advantage of its own colony or *Society in particular?* Standing thus between them both, will not the happinefs of both center in itfelf? Does not the father of a family rejoice in the happinefs both of his country and his children? But is there any colony exifting founded on thefe truly humane principles? Does not the education which the prefent colonies have received, and do ftill receive from their interefted and imprudent parents, prove the rankeft hatred between beings that ought to be united by the tendereft ties? Whence proceeds the caufe, that fmaller focieties have been compelled by mifunderftanding to feparate from the greater which gave them exiftence, but perverted education,

education, combined with the falfe principle of endeavouring to keep the child, arrived to its maturity perpetually in leading ftrings, like an infant?

Since my fhort ftay in London, I have weighed with the ftricted impartiality the argument for and againft flavery; I hope, therefore, I may be permitted to communicate my ideas on this delicate and interefting fubject, making man always the principal object of comparifon, as being the moft exact form, and the moft perfect model exifting in the creation.

No one will deny that the two diftinct and principal faculties, which effentially conftitute man, are the *Will* and the *Underftanding:* the former is derived from fome kind of love, and being from the birth poffeffed by man in common with all other animals, he would become even more favage and deftructive, if he had not the opportunity in fociety of cultivating his other faculty, the *Underftanding,* which by inftruction is capable of infinite elevation. But when

when this latter faculty comes to maturity, it then acquires a right of directing the *Will* in the way moſt conformable to wiſdom, and bears the ſame relation to it as a helm to a ſhip, which is conſtantly directed thereby in the courſe moſt favourable to the voyage.

This elevation of the *Underſtanding* above the *Will* or *Paſſions*, is the ſame as what we call *Education* or *Civilization*. Education with reſpect to every man in particular, and civilization to mankind in general.

The greateſt human ſocieties may in general be divided into two claſſes; the *civilized* and the *uncivilized*; and the obligations the former are under to the latter, are preciſely the ſame as thoſe of parents towards their children. From this analogy between children and uncivilized nations, it may then eaſily be concluded, that the one as well as the other are governed by their paſſions, in conſequence of their underſtanding not being cultivated.

If

If we feel within us an interior but diſtinct voice, dictating that we ought to ſeek our own happineſs in promoting that of our poſterity; in aſcending from particular to general, we ſhall alſo feel that the inſtructed and civilized nations for their own advantage muſt of neceſſity act unanimouſly for the happineſs of the barbarous and uncivilized.

If the tutelage of children be regarded as a period of ſlavery, I allow that the civilized nations have ſome right to exerciſe a certain dominion over the uncivilized, provided that this happy dominion be conſidered as a paternal yoke, and that the duration do not exceed the period of the child's maturity.

Let us then form new ſettlements along the African coaſt; ſettlements which ſhall have no other aim than that of inviting thoſe nations to the riches which will ariſe from the cultivation of their own country, and thence the enjoyment of civilization, to both which they are capable of applying themſelves with ardour and joy. — Let us thus on the wreck of tyranny raiſe
altars

altars to humanity. Let us give to this
weak, timid, and ignorant people, a mafcu-
line and courageous education. Let us make
them feel the nobility of their origin, that
under our tuition they may become generous
from found political intereft; and may they
no longer be flaves, but men. Let us for
our own part freely affift them in tilling the
fine country they inhabit. Let us prove to
thofe innumerable multitudes of men, by
the force of example, that they poffefs the
moft fertile foil. Let us alfo, by example,
teach them no longer to fuffer themfelves to
be torn from their native fhores. Let us
teach them to fhake off the irons, and to
revenge themfelves on the blind tyrants, who
fhackle them, by becoming more ufeful to
them in a ftate of freedom.

Note to Sec. III. *and Chap.* I.

The following Circumſtance is related by
Mr. *de la Blancherie,* from an *Extract of
the Journal of his Voyages,* publiſhed at
Paris, in 2 vols. 1775.*

A N inhabitant of St. Domingo had a negro, who for a long time had ſolicited for
his liberty, and which he had fully merited
by his ſervices; but that which ought to
have procured it for him, was preciſely what

---

* This journal gives the hiſtory of a young man whom
the author knew to have died, in conſequence of a very diſ-
ſolute life, induced from a faulty education, and from which
the moſt important deductions may be made, reſpecting
publick education, and the duty of parents. The ſame
Mr. *de la Blancherie* has, ſince the publication of this work,
digeſted and carried into execution in Paris, the plan of a
*Bureau de correſpondance générale et gratuite pour les Sciences
et les Arts,* where men of all nations, and every claſs, ſhould
find, as in *a living Encyclopedia,* (to uſe the happy expreſſion
of His Royal Highneſs the Duke of Glouceſter) the means
of communication and inſtruction, and every good office re-
lative to the Seiences and the Arts. For twelve years paſt he
has contended with all poſſible obſtacles, in order to perſuade
mankind to purſue their true intereſts, by a *reciprocation of
good offices.* Mr. *de la Blancherie* is at preſent, and will remain ſome time in England, to acquire connexions uſeful to
this grand view.

prevented

prevented his mafter from granting it, namely,
his being effentially ufeful to him. The more
the negro preffed to obtain his freedom, which
had been promifed him, the more pretences
were found for eluding and deferring the execution of the promife; the mafter himfelf no
longer hid from his flave his great attachment to him. Yet flattering as this kind of
refufal was, far from diminifhing his defire
of liberty, it ferved to encreafe it. He refolved then to employ another means, which
was to buy his freedom; appreciating himfelf according to the reafons his mafter had
given him, for not fulfilling his promife.
In fome parts of St. Domingo, the inhabitants do not enter into the detail of the food
and clothing of their negroes. They give
them two hours in a day for cultivating a
certain portion of land, granted to them for
their fubfiftence; thofe who are induftrious,
not only obtain what is neceffary, but even
that which enables them to carry on a commerce, more or lefs confiderable, according
to their ability. Our black, at the end
of fome years, gained more money than was
requifite to redeem himfelf, and prefenting
the

the gold to his mafter, told him that he was refolved to gain his liberty, and offered to pay the price of another negro. The planter furprized, fays to him, " Go, I have fuffi- " ciently trafficked in my fellow-creatures, " enjoy what is your own : you have re- " ftored me to myfelf." He immediately fold his plantation, and only remained long enough at St. Domingo to collect his proper- ty. He returned to France, and in the way to his province, was obliged to pafs through Paris. Remaining in that feductive town, he fpared nothing that could give an idea of that opulence which is attached to the name of an *American*. Women, high living, gaming, parties of pleafure of all kinds, he gave himfelf up to, without re- ftraint, embracing every opportunity of ex- pence. His fortune was foon diffipated. In that wretched fituation, it was neceffary to determine on fomething, but on what was the queftion. To remain in France a ruined man was impoffible ; to return to the iflands, what an embarraffing humiliation. Never- thelefs, on reflection, he flattered himfelf he fhould find more refources there than elfewhere,

elfewhere, depending rather on the attachment of thofe whofe fortunes he had
made in St. Domingo, than on the friend-
fhip of thofe who had been the promoters of
his ruin in France, he determined to embark.
His arrival at the Cape furprized every body
acquainted with his misfortune. They pitied
him, but no one gave him the leaft affiftance.
His ancient friends only permitted him to be
a witnefs of the pleafures he had procured
them, without making him a partaker in
their enjoyments. Many who had perfonal
obligations to him, were never at home when
he vifited them; a dreadful example this,
joined to many others which prefent themfelves daily, and are yet infufficient to prevent men from defiring to form fuch connexions. Thus reduced to live in the
wretched inns on the port, which are only
fuited to the pooreft, he had not yet been
to fee his negro; whether he had been
prevented from not knowing where he was,
or from being afhamed of prefenting himfelf in the condition to which he was reduced, I know not; but the black, who had a
houfe, having learnt his misfortune, and dif-

E

covered

covered his retreat, foon threw himfelf at the feet of his dear mafter and benefactor (for thefe were the terms he made ufe of) accompanied with tears at confidering his fituation. His zeal was not confined to words, he made him mafter in his houfe; but on reflection, putting himfelf in his place, he faw his felf-love mortified by the contempt infeparable from indigence, and the pain which is induced by the confcioufnefs of being in a ftate of dependance; he felt all the weight his benefits muft have on a generous and liberal mind. "My dear mafter," faid he, embracing his knees, "I owe to you "all I am; difpofe of every thing I have, "quit this country, where your paft mif- "fortunes will give birth to new ones; "abandon thofe ungrateful people whom "you did not oblige with a view to their "future fervices." How fhall I be able to live in France? "Ah, my dear mafter, fhall "your flave be happy enough to induce you "to accept of a tribute of his gratitude? "will you do him that kindnefs?" The mafter quite affected, knew not how to anfwer. The negro continued, "fifteen "hundred

" hundred livres, will that be fufficient ?"
Ah, it will certainly be too much anfwered
the mafter, diffolved in tears. Immediately
the black quitted him, and returning, put into
his poffeffion a deed, which infured him for
life fifteen hundred livres. The planter is
now in France, and actually receives every
year his penfion, fix months in advance.
The negro's name is Lewis Defrouleaux,
and I faw him at the Cape, where he continued to keep houfe.

F I N I S.

ADVERTISEMENT.

The Author has lately publifhed two VIEWS of the
COAST of GUINEA, with feparate Defcriptions, em-
bellifhed with four fmall Prints.—In thefe Views are introduced fome hiftorical facts related in this pamphlet, pages 9,
11, & 12. The fize 22 inches by 17, and the price 15 s.—
His view, in undertaking to publifh them, was more effen-
tially to ferve the caufe of humanity, and he has therefore
offered them at the fame price which they coft him, not
wifhing to have any emolument from this fale.—They are
to be had of the Author, No. 6, in the Poultry; at Mr. J.
Phillips's, George-Yard, Lombard-Street; Mr. B. Evans,
Printfeller, in the Poultry; Mr. S. Walter, Homer's Head,
Charing-Crofs; Mr. W. Dickinfon, Printfeller, No. 158,
New-Bond-Street; Meff. Robfon and Clarke, New-Bond-
Street; and Mr. B. Chaftanier, No. 62, Tottenham-
Court-Road.

CONTENTS.

SECT. IV.

Defcription of the Coaft.

SECT. V.

Of the Impediments which will oppofe the European Settlements on the Coaft of Guinea.

SECT. VI.

E R R A T U M.

Page 13, Line 16, for lum, read Salum.

www.ingramcontent.com/pod-product-compliance
Lightning Source LLC
Chambersburg PA
CBHW020331090426
42735CB00009B/1489